A gift for

_____

from

_____

At the HEART of MOTHERHOOD

Designed by: Walé Adeniran
Art Director: Mark Cordes
Editorial Development: Jane-Elyse Pryor

Contributing writers: Keely Chace, John Dill, Renee Duvall, Russ Ediger, Steve Finken, Jennifer Fujita,
Cheryl Gaines, Debby Glasgow, Bill Gray, Carolyn Hoppe, Jim Howard, Pam Kelley, Barbara Loots,
Laurie Monsees, Tina Neidlein, Ginnie Job, Lisa Riggin, Dee Ann Stewart, Sharon Valleau, Dean Walley

Printed and bound in China

BOK 4097

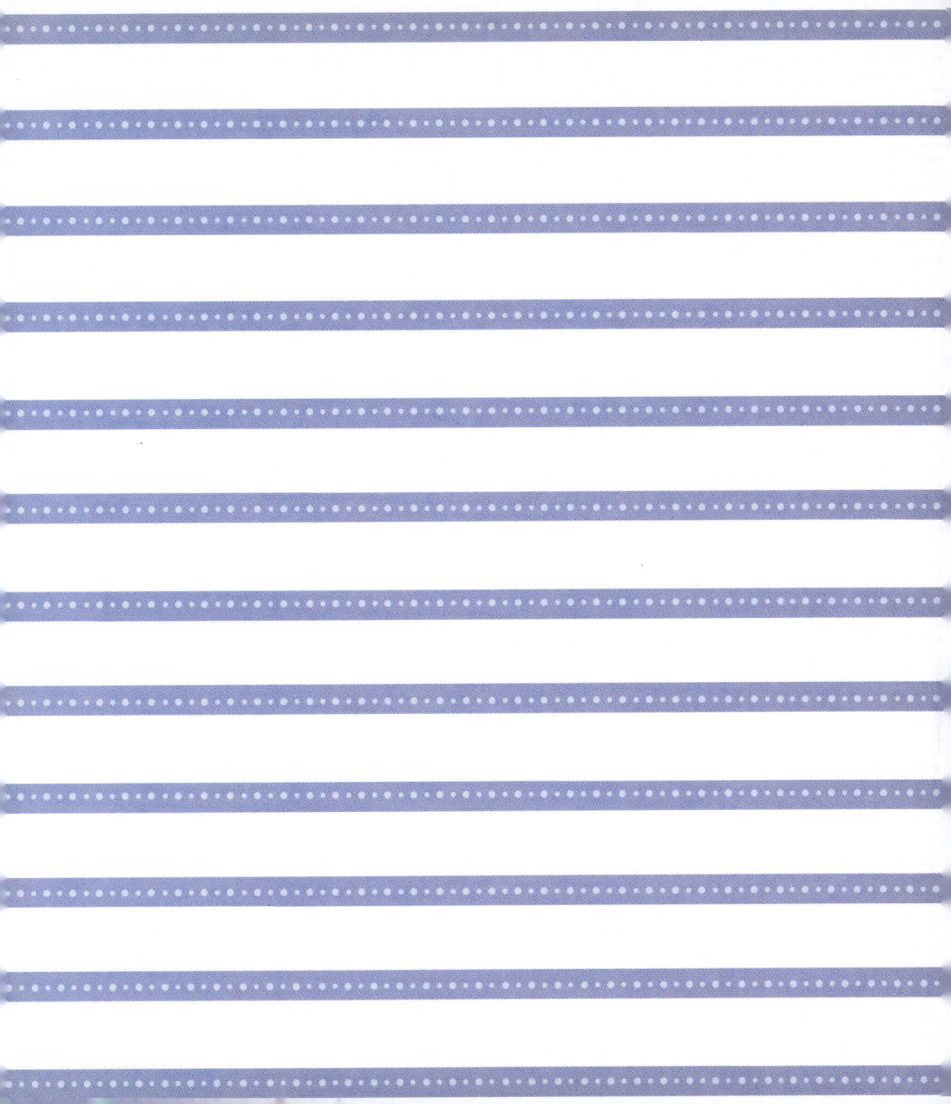

At the HEART
of MOTHERHOOD

Motherhood...

the boldest move

a woman can make,

the most challenging

step she can take,

the dearest gift

she can give.

Keely Chace

"Mother" and "love"...

different words,

same meaning.

They both

work miracles.

Motherhood...
    ...love begins and ends there.
        Robert Browning

A mother's love is measured
not in moments of time
but in timeless moments.

*Of course
there's such a thing
as angels.
Only sometimes
they don't have wings...
and we call them
mothers.*

❦

Flowers have the sun,

and children have their mothers.

In motherhood,

the heart gives unconditionally,

loves eternally.

A mother's love
is a favorite song,
playing softly,
steadily, constantly
in the hearts
of her children.

Mothers weave the beauty of love into our lives.

There's
only one thing
that can make you feel
warmer and safer
than a blanket...
Mother.

At the heart of motherhood...

...is "interruptibility!"

Debby Glasgow

*A mother sees
through eyes of love
and listens
with her heart.*

In all nature there is no beauty to compare with the beauty of a mother's love.

At the heart of motherhood...

...is the kind of satisfaction
unequalled in any other
profession on Earth.

Tina Neidlein

A mother's love

is a map for living,

for making the right turns,

avoiding the rough roads,

and arriving safely

wherever you go.

At the heart of motherhood...

...is the kind
of love a woman
can find only
when she becomes
a mother...
totally unconditional,
unselfih,
undeniably genuine.

Cheryl Gaines

*From the beginning
a mother is writing
a poem of life,
composing a song of joy,
and creating a miracle
that will make
the world brand new
again.*

Dean Walley

❧

To be a mother

is to fill

the smallest things

with love

and place them gently

in a tiny hand

and a tiny heart

for safekeeping.

❧

All the reassurance
that a child
would ever need
is written
on a mother's face.

*The mother's heart
is the child's schoolroom.*

Henry Ward Beecher

At the heart of motherhood...

...is an ever-changing relationship

between a mother and her child.

I was surprised when my daughter

was born that our relationship

was so dynamic—with every growth

and change she went through,

I went through my own,

and our relationship evolved with us.

Pam Kelley

A mother's love
runs like a vine through a lifetime,
and every sweet, unselfish act
becomes an unfolding leaf
of character and goodness.

At the heart of motherhood...

...is the joy
of making a difference
in a life
by loving, guiding, teaching
and encouraging the gifts
our children have.

Leslie Baugher

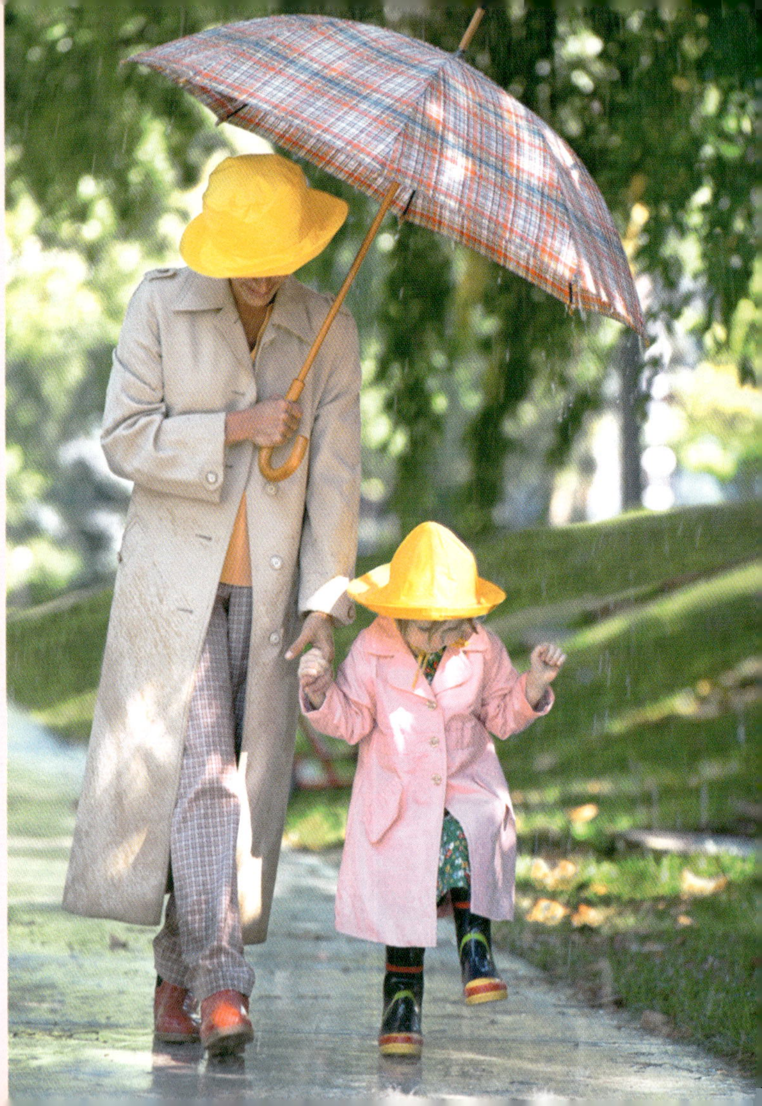

Never underestimate the power of a mother's love.

*Motherhood brings
both sunshine and rain,
and we welcome both
into our lives—
knowing deep down
it's the only way
to make a rainbow.*

At the heart of motherhood...

...is endless patience–
for kids, tying shoelaces,
spreading peanut butter,
brushing their teeth.
When a mom really wants to yell,
"HURRY UP,"
she learns to smile and say instead,
"Great job. You did it!"

Laurie Monsees

Motherhood is vigorous, mysterious, astonishing work.

There are ways of looking at life

that only a mother can teach you.

At the heart of motherhood...

...you will find a mother's heart.

Bill Gray

*Mother is the anchor
that grounds us,
and from there
we reach,
we explore,
we grow,
safe in the knowledge
that we are truly loved,
always understood.*

At the heart of motherhood...

*...is a sheltering fierceness
that cannot be explained,
only felt, whenever our children
reach out to us in need.*

Lisa Riggin

We're given only one heart

and one mother to show us

what it's there for.

At the heart of motherhood...

...is hope, stronger than doubt,
that your children will feel loved...
hope, stronger than fear,
that they will be safe and happy...
hope, stronger than habit,
that you will have the grace
to let them go...
and hope that someday
their own children will bring them
the immeasurable joy
yours have given you.

Ginnie Job